The CHINESE BOOK of ANIMAL POWERS

Chungliang Al Huang

JOANNA COTLER BOOKS

An Imprint of HarperCollinsPublishers

Love

The Chinese Book of Animal Powers Text and illustrations copyright © 1999 (The year of TWOO) by Chungliang Al Huang Printed in the U.S.A. All rights reserved.   http://www.harperchildrens.com   Library of Congress Cataloging-in-Publication Data   Huang, Chungliang Al.   The Chinese book of animal powers / by Chungliang Al Huang.   p.   cm.   "Joanna Cotler Books"   Summary: Describes the twelve animals of the Chinese zodiac with their strengths and weaknesses, and shows how to write their names in Chinese calligraphy.   ISBN 0-06-027728-9. — ISBN 0-06-027729-7 (lib. bdg.) 1. Astrology, Chinese—Juvenile literature.   2. Animals—Folklore—Juvenile literature.   [1. Astrology, Chinese.   2. Animals—Folklore.   3. Folklore.] l. Title. BF1714.C5H76 1999 99-10671 133.5'9251—dc21 CIP   Typography by Alicia Mikles   1 2 3 4 5 6 7 8 9 10 ❖ First Edition

This book is for my grandson,

Avery Yulan, who entered this world riding

the CHI powers of TSWOO year and WHOO month.

This book is also for all the children, their parents,

and grandparents, who embody the CHI powers

of all the animals on this Earth

and under Heaven.

WHAT ARE CHINESE ANIMAL POWERS? Chinese legend tells us that the lord Buddha summoned the animals to hear of their powers in his sermon under the Banyan Tree. Representing all the animals in the Kingdom, twelve creatures arrived one by one, led by TSWOO. NEEOH, WHOO, TWOO, LOHNG, SHURR, MAAH, YAANG, HOH, JEE, GOH, and JOO[1] followed. Buddha taught them about their strengths and weaknesses, then sent all twelve animals into the world to guide people in their growth, linking each animal to a month and a year.[2]

Since that time almost 2500 years ago, the Chinese have believed that each of us is born with one or two of the initial characteristics and powers of these twelve animals, depending on the month and year of our birth. As we grow, we gradually learn about the animal powers within the personalities of our family members and our friends, so that we may learn to get along better with others and be happier with ourselves.

Each of the twelve animals has its own power of creative expression, which the Chinese call CHI (pronounced *chee*). Each creature, mythical in dimension, teaches us to develop our imagination and guides us on our path, which the Chinese call TAO (pronounced *dow*), so we can become fully special human beings.

---

1. *Though their names can be translated into English, learn their Chinese names so that you remember that each animal's name stands for more than one specific animal.*
2. *You will find a chart in the back of this book so you can figure out under which animal month and year you were born.*

For example, if you were born in the *year* of LOHNG, you may identify with a positive quality of this animal, such as its charisma. But perhaps you were born in the *month* of WHOO. How do you integrate LOHNG's exuberance with WHOO's earthiness? Buddha meant the animals to be guides and to teach us about the Chinese ideas of YIN and YANG—balance. But don't be limited by your "born-with" powers; most of us have a little of each animal in our character.

In addition to its particular characteristics, each animal has its own calligraphic Chinese symbol, which you'll see often looks like the animal itself, or that animal's movement. While it is possible to translate the animals' names into English or other languages, I think it is much more fun to learn their folksy Chinese origins. I would like you to be able to see the CHI powers in the pictures of these animals, in the brush strokes that make up the calligraphy, and to pronounce their names, with the sounds tracing way back into ancient times. As you read through the book, I hope you will almost be able to see the animals dancing their unique dances and hear them speaking their special musical languages. I hope you will enjoy all the animal powers in this book and learn to grow into a special, all-powerful, happy, and creative whole person!

Chungliang Al Huang

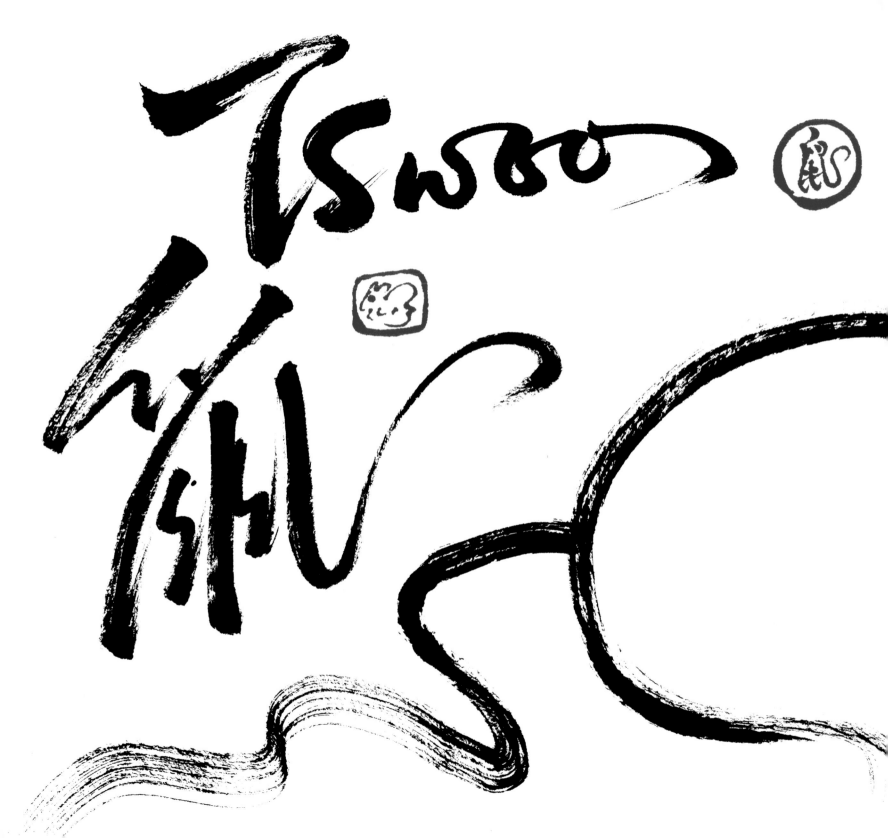

This small, quick rodent has enormous curiosity about life. Sometimes we call it a mouse, a rat, or a guinea pig, a squirrel or a chipmunk. All belong to the family of TSWOO. Legend tells us that when Buddha gave his sermon under the Banyan Tree, the bright-eyed and keen-minded TSWOO was the first to sit at Buddha's feet. TSWOO represents the fresh and innocent person with "The Beginner's Mind."

If you were born in the year or the month of TSWOO, you come into the world already smart, quick, and alert. At times you may feel small, but you can outwit any cat around. No bully can match your sharpness. You are intensely intelligent, the first to show an eagerness to learn. Be careful, though: don't let your cleverness turn to cunning. You don't need to pump yourself up to fight the big guys, but don't hide yourself away, either. Take a stand and be proud of who you are. You are persistent and patient, and you've got true grit. And you can nibble through any barrier that gets in your way.

This hardworking, dependable, mighty creature has a great capacity to absorb an abundance of knowledge. Sometimes we call it a bull, a cow, or an ox, a buffalo, or rhinoceros. Folk legend depicts NEEOH as our strong, unruly self, who needs to be tamed and put in its rightful place. In the Zen Buddhist fable, the Ox runs away from the child to play hide-and-seek, until the child learns to trace his steps, finds him, tames him, and eventually becomes one with the Ox—riding him merrily, while playing a bamboo flute.

If you were born in the year or the month of NEEOH, you are strong and responsible, and can work hard if you want to. You may seem a bit slow moving, but you are steady. You chew things over and digest everything. You will learn what the Chinese call WU WEI (pronounced *woo way*), meaning you will not get in your own way, but will let life flow smoothly. Be happy with your natural instinct to serve and carry others' weight, but don't think you will get extra sympathy and attention for your service and sacrifices. When you feel confident, you express your good ideas loudly and clearly. At times you may seem overly thoughtful, but you do not hesitate to gallop triumphantly to the front line.

This powerfully beautiful cat roars thunderously and from time to time meows sweetly. Underneath its stealthy exterior is a gentle soul who loves to be cuddled. Legend tells us that WHOO is the king of the forest and mountains, standing alone and proudly aloof.

WHOO embodies strength and agility, beauty and fear—and asks us to embrace life's challenges.

If you were born in the year or the month of WHOO, everyone adores you. But sometimes you are arrogant and vain. Learn to listen to your own voice so you can roar with truth. Consider the importance of purring with appreciation to those who love you. Take charge with your natural leadership, but avoid being bossy and conceited. There will always be other tigers who have more clout and stripes. Be smart, and pay attention to your gutsy, deeply grounded instincts.

This lightning-quick bouncer with an uplifting gait and a "toothy-smile" personality is sometimes called a rabbit and sometimes a bunny. TWOO is very clever and productive. Legend tells us that once upon a time in the Celestial Sky, TWOO, a resident of the moon, was appointed by the Immortals to be the "Good News" messenger. And because of its fondness for tasting scented herbs, fragrant flowers, and vegetables, TWOO was put in charge of preparing Buddhist banquets. On the clear full-moon nights when we look up into the silvery disk, we may still see TWOO joyfully preparing delicious morsels for heavenly feasts.

If you were born in the year or the month of TWOO, you are clever, speedy, and enthusiastic, and you are capable of producing great works in life. But don't run too fast too soon, or you'll miss all the real fun along the way. You are already way ahead. Keep your mind on the present, so you won't miss out on all the wonderful moments in life. TWOO teaches us that "faster" or "more" is not always better, and that "well done" is always "soon enough."

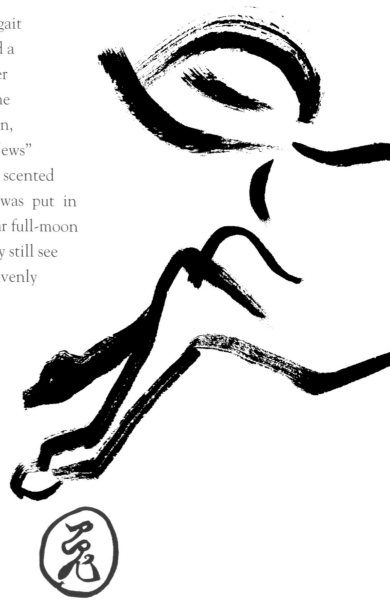

This mythical dragon can live at the bottom of the sea, on land, and fly high in the sky. It has fish scales, giant eagle claws, antelope horns, and eyes of a tiger, and puffs out fireballs as bright as giant, illuminating golden pearls. It is the imperial symbol of China, with its powerful five claws representing Fire, Water, Wood, Metal, and Earth, the cosmic energy Chinese call CHI. In tune with Heaven and Earth, LOHNG is constantly and magically transforming.

If you were born in the year or the month of LOHNG, you are born special—a natural leader. However, your charisma and uniqueness can appear overwhelming to others. There are many things you can do well—

sometimes too many—so you may not be able to integrate all your outward talents properly. Avoid the trap of being a show-off, or you'll steal another's thunder. Go deep inside yourself; learn to appreciate your inner need to constantly grow and change. If you wish to be looked up to, honor others: earn your specialness. LOHNG shows us we can adapt, change, and transform—and fly high.

Shurr

This serpentine creature travels like wind and water, fluid and slick as a whistle without any need of "pumping-iron" legs. Outwardly it may seem slippery and menacing, but the soul-searching SHURR requires quiet time to coil up inwardly in hibernation, groggy and oblivious to the commotion of the world. Legend tells about a silvery SHURR meditating in the deep mountains for centuries, in order to attain the magical power to become anything and anyone it wishes to be. SHURR differs from LOHNG in that its transformative power is derived from long years of discipline, earned by hard work.

If you were born in the year or the
month of SHURR, you enter the world
colorful and quick in action, intelligent and agile in
thought. But because you seem wiggly and undefined, you can stir up trouble and get
away with plenty. Be careful, or the magic you conjure up may work against you. So be sure
the tricks you invent are for the common good. And use humor to slip out of your own
schemes. SHURR helps us wake up to our brightest
ideas, reach for our highest intelligence.
As SHURR sheds old skin to renew
and redeem itself, so can you.

This robustly imposing animal gallops and neighs, its handsome mane dancing in the wind. Legend tells us about the graceful MAAH disrupting order in Heaven with its boundless free spirit. So the Immortals reluctantly clipped its wings to contain its passionate abandonment, and decided to put MAAH into human service to help speed up and carry along the plodding creatures on Earth. Sometimes humans try to harness it by putting a bit in its mouth, a rein around its neck, and a saddle on its back to squash its wild nature. But MAAH is most beautiful when it is free and wild. MAAH is the original "Winged Spirit" of creativity.

If you were born in the year or the month of MAAH, your true nature is to run and jump and be naturally wild. You hate to be tied down, but it does feel good to help out and be useful—except when you're too saddled with everybody else's load. Since it is your destiny to carry and guide others, learn the skills to inspire them, so they can share the excitement and be a free spirit with you. Feel the wind as you gallop through life and set everyone free!

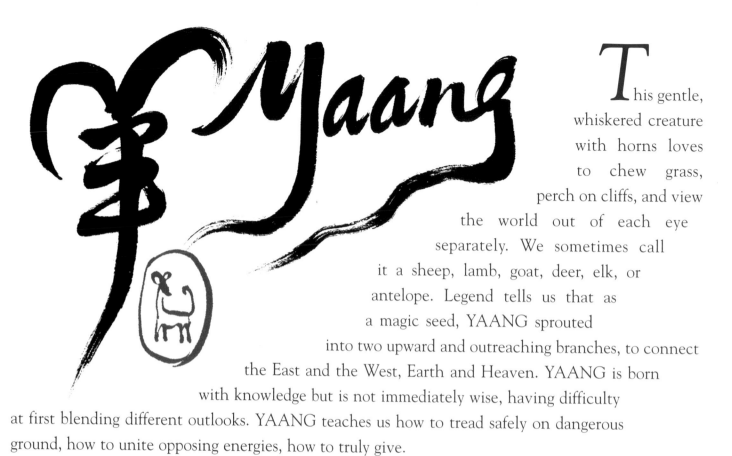

Yaang

This gentle, whiskered creature with horns loves to chew grass, perch on cliffs, and view the world out of each eye separately. We sometimes call it a sheep, lamb, goat, deer, elk, or antelope. Legend tells us that as a magic seed, YAANG sprouted into two upward and outreaching branches, to connect the East and the West, Earth and Heaven. YAANG is born with knowledge but is not immediately wise, having difficulty at first blending different outlooks. YAANG teaches us how to tread safely on dangerous ground, how to unite opposing energies, how to truly give.

If you were born in the year or the month of YAANG, you begin your life as a contented person, comfortable with at least two views of life and of yourself. At your best, you're balanced and enjoy being a well-rounded person, but you thrive in challenging situations, often suspended on the high end of the seesaw. You are a born nurturer, always delighted to share your wealth with others; but because you are generous, others may take advantage of you. Be aware that you are always balancing—and trust yourself.

This most humanlike animal can do almost everything we do except talk and compute. It swings on trees better than the best trapeze artists, and makes fun of our follies with utter honesty.

To enter the world with HOH, it is easy to pretend to see, hear, and speak no evil, and to appear the perfect angel. The Monkey King is the most beloved character in China because he is so like all of us, possessing our best and worst qualities. Legend tells us he made Heaven playful, brazenly challenging the Immortals, who undermined his vain need to always win. Because of HOH's arrogance, he was imprisoned under the mighty hand of the Buddha, deep inside the "Five Fingers Mountain" (symbolizing the Five Elements of Nature: Fire, Water, Wood, Metal, Earth) to repent and meditate for a long period of time.

If you were born in the year or the month of HOH, you can be funny, delightful, and brilliant. But you can also be a royal pain with your vain antics. You cannot sit still long enough to accomplish anything at hand, and you detest being told, "Not now, later!" You are a born performer, mimic, show-off, clown. Learn to listen to those you respect, slow down, and study from teachers you admire. Humility is a true challenge for you. Once you manage to settle down, you will be a sure winner. HOH distinguishes for us the difference between quick tricks and the true magic of life.

*L*egend
tells us about this winged creature, a mythical bird who became so
obsessed with its natural beauty, it spent hours vainly pluming its gorgeous feathers. JEE was so
happy being adored that it settled for the measly food offerings in front of its beak, neglecting
the daily practice of strengthening its flying power, until one day its wings failed to
soar. When JEE learned to regain its original great visions from the highest
branches of the Tree of Life, its life journey began.

If you were born in the year or the month of JEE, like MAAH, you
are by nature a winged spirit. A person with high ideals, you often get
bogged down by everyday routines. You are easily enticed into ventures that satisfy
you momentarily but lack substance and staying power. Your deep inner wish is to do
something meaningful that would require careful planning and discipline. Because you yearn
for the vast sky and open horizon, you can
be a wonderful daydreamer.

Be the genuine star of your own show, more for your own sake than for the applause. If you put your heart and mind to it, you can get things done, enjoy what's right here, and still manage to spread your wings whenever and wherever you want.

We call it "man's best friend." But before we made it depend on us, it was wild and free as a wolf, coyote, or fox roaming in wilderness, howling at the moon. Legend tells us GOH was once the most keenly sensitive creature in the universe, with no fewer than twelve senses. GOH was the best and most reliable sniffer, taster, feeler, senser, and intuitor in the Celestial Kingdom. Because of GOH's sensitivity and need for constant strokes from the Immortals, it was banished to Earth to wander the wild, fated to search for homey human comfort.

If you were born in the year or the Month of GOH, you are sensitive and affectionate by nature. You come alive and thrive outdoors, by the campfire, basking under the sun, or glowing beneath the full moon. You may enjoy sheltered comfort, but you cannot be cooped up inside for long. You love people and thrive on kindness; appreciate being cared for but hate being patronized. You have a natural instinct to guide others to the right paths, but avoid being humorless. Cultivate a true zest for life and inspire others to the same. Being often right on target and usually extremely helpful to others makes you happy. GOH represents our natural instincts and the most affectionate and trustworthy qualities in all of us.

*T*his easygoing and sassy creature enjoys life in the here and now, and is unassumingly wise. JOO may seem slow and dense at times, but is actually very smart, realistic, and fun loving. JOO is contented and quietly interested in the cultivation of the heart and soul. Legend tells us JOO was the most lovable and esteemed animal in the Celestial Garden, a downright homey philosopher with few words but admirable deeds and actions. When the Great Buddha gave his Banyan Tree Sermon, JOO was the last to arrive, getting there perfectly on time, cool and unruffled, at full attention to receive the teaching.

If you were born in the year or the month of JOO, you enjoy life as a full banquet. You take time to partake and savor life's many offerings, without having to hurry through or become anxious. You don't understand why people compete and hoard, since all good things in life always come when you are truly ready. You are content to be a late bloomer, because deep inside you feel perfectly okay to be who you are. So if everybody else is making a big deal, rushing around working furiously to impress, you can just let things ride and trust that your moment to shine will come. You know the life in front of you is the real one. So, take your time to wallow in the comforting warm mud and enjoy life's pleasures. But don't get too lazy. Once in a while, go into the field to smell the flowers, drink the nectar, and dance with the butterflies. JOO is a lesson in what the Chinese call the TAO of Being instead of Doing.

Dancing Glossary

A great way to learn about the animal powers is to draw the animals and their symbols—and the best way to learn to draw them is to dance them. Enjoy tracing the energy patterns of the Chinese brush strokes that echo the movements and the graceful dance of these animals. You need to explore and embody their dance by moving. Begin by tracing these flowing line patterns, and notice how they somehow all come together with a compact, dynamic final flourish. Imagine a quick sketch artist drawing you as you dance around expressing fully your CHI powers, with your free, uninhibited, very unique personal moves. You will be amazed to recognize how many distinctive qualities of these animals are represented in your CHI movements.

CHI is the primal life energy in all creatures, and the force between Heaven and Earth. CHI is the breath of the Earth, the movement in our bodies, the dance of our feelings and our thoughts. CHI connects us with everywhere and everything, and lives in our deepest inner selves. It is the primal force of our lives.

YIN and YANG are the two halves of a moving, balancing whole, which is called TAI JI. Every animal/person has a fair amount of both YIN/YANG qualities in order to become a well-rounded, happy TAI JI individual.

TAI

JI

YIN/YANG

CHI

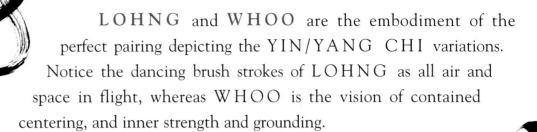

LOHNG

LOHNG and WHOO are the embodiment of the perfect pairing depicting the YIN/YANG CHI variations. Notice the dancing brush strokes of LOHNG as all air and space in flight, whereas WHOO is the vision of contained centering, and inner strength and grounding.

Chinese call TAO the Way of Life according to nature. See how the calligraphy looks like someone settling happily on a boat, floating down the river.

WU WEI is staying out of your way, knowing not to interfere with nature or your path. The picture of WU shows the process of a natural forest fire, to create a clearing for new growth. The picture of WEI shows a wild and free-spirited horse being harnessed to be reined under the rider's controlling will.

WHOO

TAO

WU

WEI

Year and Month Chart

 Tswoo

J A N U A R Y

2008	1996	1984
1972	1960	1948
1936	1924	1912

 Lohng

M A Y

2012	2000	1988
1976	1964	1952
1940	1928	1916

 Hoh

S E P T E M B E R

2016	2004	1992
1980	1968	1956
1944	1932	1920

 Neeoh

F E B R U A R Y

2009	1997	1985
1973	1961	1949
1937	1925	1913

 shurr

J U N E

2013	2001	1989
1977	1965	1953
1941	1929	1917

 Jee

O C T O B E R

2017	2005	1993
1981	1969	1957
1945	1933	1921

 Whoo

M A R C H

2010	1998	1986
1974	1962	1950
1938	1926	1914

Maahs

J U L Y

2014	2002	1990
1978	1966	1954
1942	1930	1918

Goh

N O V E M B E R

2018	2006	1994
1982	1970	1958
1946	1934	1922

 Twooo

A P R I L

2011	1999	1987
1975	1963	1951
1939	1927	1915

 Yaang

A U G U S T

2015	2003	1991
1979	1967	1955
1943	1931	1919

Jooo

D E C E M B E R

2019	2007	1995
1983	1971	1959
1947	1935	1923